BACK ROW BRIGHTON

CINEMA-GOING
IN BRIGHTON & HOVE

QueenSpark Books

Dedicated to Dave Huggins
1926 – 2008

Published by QueenSpark Books
© QueenSpark Books, 2009

QueenSpark is a non-profit making community publishing
and writing organisation, which has helped the people of
Brighton & Hove tell their stories since 1972.

QueenSpark Books
Room 211
University of Brighton
10-11 Pavilion Parade
Brighton BN2 1RA
Tel. 01273 571710
www.queensparkbooks.org.uk
www.thedeckchair.org.uk

ISBN: 9780904733361

A catalogue record of this book is available from the British Library.

QueenSpark has made every effort to ensure that the content of this publication
is accurate, but takes no responsibility for errors or omissions herein. However we
do welcome any feedback or clarification for consideration for future reprints.

Typeset in Chaparral Pro and Gill Sans 11 / 14

CONTENTS

ACKNOWLEDGEMENTS

Managing Editors
Sarah Hutchings
John Riches

Writers
Amy Riley
Martin Payne
Frank Flood

Contributors
Jimmy Anderson
Harry Atkins
Patrick Collins
Raymond (Dickie) Bird
Roy Grant
Peter Groves
Dave Huggins
Len Leichti
John Wall
Young writers from the Little
Green Pig writing project

Art Director
Nigel French

Cover Design
Joe Luxton
Becky Parnell
Claude d'Avoine

Designers
Alice Marshall
Sue Craig
Theresa May
Vicki Williams

Editors
Sheila McWattie
Debbie Waldon
Robert Loughrey
Lauren Lumby
Donna Hetherington
Catherine Page

Sarah Windebank
Adam Whitehall
Roslyn Cook
Teresa Cairns
Julie Singleton

Research
Matthew May
Jen Sanders

Interviewers
Anton Collins
Jamie Sellers
Sarah Cross
Vicky Heape
Teresa Lipson
Catherine Page
Birdie Johnson
Ella Burns
Amy Riley
Janet Holm

Interviewees
Peter Chitty
Geraldine Curran
Mike Lang
Beverley Lee
Billy Lee
Diana Meeten
Bryan Moody
Rodney Patterson

Photographs
Dusashenka
Harry Atkins
Peter Bailey
Paul Bland
Trevor Chepstow
Royal Pavilion and
Museums, Brighton & Hove
Chris Horlock
Philip Howard
Robert Jeeves

Additional Photography
Henry Bruce
Sue Craig

**Thanks to all these people
who have helped in the
making of this book**
Stella Cardus
Chris Harrison
Nigel French
Henry Bruce
Tricia Leonard
Tom Sawyer
Melita Dennett
Kevin Bacon
Jenny Hand
Beverley Green
Jennifer Drury at
mybrightonandhove.org.uk
Tim Brown
Frank Gray
James Tully at
Kingswest Odeon
Colin Dibley
Debbie Chepstow
Thanks to Brighton & Sussex
Community Knowledge
Exchange (BSCKE) at the
University of Brighton for
funding the Talking Pictures
project, some interview
material from which
was used in this book.

INTRODUCTION

Rather than a being a straightforward account of cinema history, *Back Row Brighton* is an homage to cinema, and particularly cinema-going in the city.

Continuing its tradition of 'telling the tales of Brighton & Hove' QueenSpark presents an affectionate look at some of the city's 'lost cinemas' and includes personal recollections from many of its older residents who tell of the dancing, the excitement, the queues and the scale and beauty of these picture houses – all evoking a forgotten world, very fondly remembered.

The glitz and glamour offered by the films of Hollywood in the middle of the last century were a brief and affordable escape from austerity – or not so brief, in the case of those who told us that they often stayed to watch the same film over and over.

Somewhere around the 1960s, the increase in television take-up, coupled with an increase in lesser-quality films, signalled the death-knell for mass attendance at the cinema. This is when many of the glorious buildings fell into disrepair. A social phenomenon was on the wane, and QueenSpark feels bound to share many of the fond memories held by its residents.

QueenSpark Books is committed to offering local residents the experience of working on its publications and *Back Row Brighton* is no exception. The text, interviews, picture research (including the taking of many new photographs), editing, layout and cover design have all been carried out by QueenSpark volunteers. It is thanks to their enthusiasm, generosity and commitment that *Back Row Brighton* has been published. Many thanks to them all, and on their behalf we hope you enjoy the book. – **QueenSpark Books**

MARTIN PAYNE

THE
ACADEMY

1911–1973

LAST FILM SCREENED
Peter Bogdanovich's *The Last Picture Show*.

DID YOU KNOW?
The Academy was open for thirteen years
before sound was installed in 1929.

THE ACADEMY USED TO BE ON THE EASTERN SIDE OF West Street, where Yates Wine Lodge currently stands. Opened in June 1911, it remained for over sixty years one of the City's most successful cinemas. This was despite intense competition from the nearby Regent in Queens Road, Prince's in North Street and the Queens Electric, also in West Street.

Originally a Turkish bath house called the Brighton Hammam, which had stood on the site since 1868, the Academy opened with a seating capacity for 400 people. However, subsequent refurbishments and modernisations finally increased that number to over 1,000, and the Moorish décor it had kept for many years was eventually replaced by an art deco design.

While throughout its long history it often had to make do with second-run screenings, showing films already played elsewhere, it was amongst the first cinemas in town to introduce 'talking pictures' in the late 1920s. In the early 1930s the Academy experimented with programmes that heavily featured newsreels, and was thus briefly renamed Tatler News Theatre.

It was under its original name however, that it prospered for decades, finally closing on 24 January 1973. Its owners at that time, the Rank Organisation, had decided to shut it down as work neared completion on its Odeon cinema in the Kingswest complex. The building was demolished in 1975.

Birth of Flowers was shown as one of a programme of films on the Academy's opening night and it is entirely fitting that its final screening was the Peter Bogdanovich film *The Last Picture Show*.

Outside the Academy, date unknown

THE ROYAL PAVILION AND MUSEUMS, BRIGHTON & HOVE

West Street circa 1950. The Academy can be seen on the left

At the Academy in West Street an attendant used to come round squirting disinfectant from a huge syringe. Hard luck if you happened to get the full blast – they were never careful. The Academy's cheap seats were at the front of the auditorium, as was the entrance to the men's toilets. Every time that brass-railed door swung open the smell wafting in made your hair stand on end. – **Dave Huggins**

The first one I went to with my husband, on our first date, was the Academy in West Street and we saw *White Christmas* with Bing Crosby and Danny Kaye. – **Diana Meeten**

My friends and I started going to dances. Mostly at the Regent or Corn Exchange. And we really enjoyed skating. We met a few members of the opposite sex, but none of us had any serious affairs. We also frequented the cinemas when we could afford it. The Odeon, Savoy, The Regent, or the dear old Academy. They always had the films after the rest and we always went there to see one we had missed, we could get in for nine pence. – **Olive Masterson**, *The Circle of Life*, 1986. **QueenSpark Books**

We only stayed in the one night a week, other nights were spent going to the various cinemas. We had a good number then. There was the Odeon in West Street, the Odeon in Kemptown, the Academy, Gaiety and the Regent. There were others, some of which we called 'flea pits', which showed only old films. The larger places in the centre of town showed the latest films, so you could see a different one every night of the week if you wished. – **Leila Abrahams,** *Me and My Mum*, 1996. **QueenSpark Books**

The Academy was a small hall cinema; it had room enough for about 400 people. You went through the main doors; straight opposite you was a kiosk, run by a lovely lady whose name I can't remember, unfortunately she's probably not with us anymore. There were two doors either side and a small circle, so it was a fairly intimate theatre and very nice too. Again, it shouldn't have been knocked down it would have done now as a rep cinema like, for foreign films that are very popular at the Duke of York's. It's a sad shame that's gone.

The Academy, 1935

TREVOR CHEPSTOW

A staff fire drill at
the Academy Cinema
circa 1949-1950

They used to get short runs of things, the one with
Maggie Smith about the teacher was on for a long while,
and they used to get the third only Odeon release, which
used to be the Gaumont release, so they got the rather
inferior product and it was there that we had the kids' show
on Saturday mornings. So the Odeon would get the number
one product, The Academy would get the number two or
the number three product and the Regent would get the
blockbusters basically.

For the kids' matinees I used to get people up. We had a
competition for a pop group or singers and various other
competitions I'd try and run for that. But the Academy had
no proper stage and we had to do it below the screen, but it
still worked, it was fine.

It was a big uphill fight in the 1960s to get people into
the cinema. The only films that really worked were the
big, big blockbusters. The second and third release on our
Rank chain, it was hard to fill a cinema sometimes with
them, even the small Academy. Rank's idea was to get a
family audience in to see family movies. Mr Deutsch and
his other people, the Rank people, didn't like the idea of
people sitting through horror films. But when they saw,
for instance, the take for *House of Wax* with Vincent Price,
which showed at the Savoy, they knew how much money

each cinema had taken, although how they knew I do not know, even on the other chains, but they changed their minds in the end and there were x films that used to go to the Academy, not the main Odeon and not, definitely not, the Regent.' – **Mike Lang, former Manager of The Academy**

Talking about horror films, there used to be the Academy in West Street and if you went on a Sunday they used to have the Hammer Horror films and Vincent Price films and then you'd get the yobbos go and start making fun of it. So you'd get all this catcalling going on, especially if there was a bit that was so over the top, like Vincent Price in *The Pit and the Pendulum*. I think you just joined in. I think cinema has got very serious now, hasn't it? It's much more expensive, unless you go to the Silver Screen. – **Geraldine Curran**

I worked in the Academy down in West Street – that was a very small cinema built on the site of some old baths, and it was most creepy – if you went downstairs at night to put all the lighting out, it was all these old tunnels, and it smelt horribly of damp – you had to have a torch with you to make sure you could see your way out again … We used to have films running for four, five, six, seven weeks at a time … *The Ten Commandments* (1956) was one of them – we did the first run of that in Brighton – you could almost recite the dialogue off by heart, you'd heard it so many times. – **Peter Chitty**

The Academy – that used to be a Turkish bath – when it closed it still had gas secondary lighting – it was a really old, musty theatre with torn curtains – but it was the friendliest of the theatres to be in. – **John (former projectionist)**

FRANK FLOOD

THE ADVENTURES OF JANE

FEATURING THE GAIETY CINEMA

(1937–1980)

DID YOU KNOW?

The Gaiety Cinema on Lewes Road, Brighton was
known later as The Ace, Vogue and Classic cinema.

Exterior. Top of Queens Road, outside Brighton station. Day. Two villains are standing in front of the station concourse, finalising their plans while awaiting the arrival of the 'protagonist'.

Previous Page:
The Gaiety, circa 1936

THE SCENE IS FROM a late-1940s black-and-white movie, Brighton-based, shot on various locations around the town. *Brighton Rock*, surely? Well, no. It's actually from *The Adventures of Jane*, a low-budget 1949 attempt by the nascent Brighton Studios to cash in on the already waning popularity of the *Daily Mirror* strip cartoon. Instead of the fate meted out to the unfortunate Fred Hale in the opening section of the Boulting brothers' film, the worst that happens to our heroine when her train gets in is that she loses her skirt in a slammed door and has to cover her (doubtless off-ration) silk undies with the chief villain's overcoat.

On almost every level, *The Adventures of Jane* is a remarkably awful film. The plot – involving a jewelled bracelet that may or may not be fake, an apparently Anglo-American gang of thieves and shysters, and a heroine whose major talent is for losing articles of clothing – is the sort of farrago that would shame a daytime American TV soap. The acting ranges from wooden (most of the cast) to painfully overripe (Peter Butterworth in an early appearance as a 'comic' drunk; Wally Patch – later a mainstay of much of Ken Loach's TV work – as a lipsmackingly lecherous customs officer). The dialogue is often either inane or incomprehensible, and sometimes both; the direction is so pedestrian that both the 'comedy' and 'thriller' aspects of the movie repeatedly fall flat. In all these respects, it seems extraordinary that Jane is now available in a DVD series labelled as *The Best of British Collection*.

And yet … bad films, like bad records, can often be at least as evocative as good ones. For all its awfulness as a movie, *The Adventures of Jane* is a treasure-trove of historical, sociological and topographic insights. Several writers – notably Steve Chibnall and Andy Medhurst – have analysed Brighton's repeated appearance in British films as a narrative terminus, an end-of-the-road/line/pier location yielding either death and disillusion (*Brighton Rock* itself, of course; but also *Jigsaw*, *Villain*, *Quadrophenia*, *Mona Lisa*,

Dirty Weekend, London to Brighton) or an uncorseted escape from mundane routine (*Penny Points to Paradise, Genevieve, Carry On at Your Convenience*). What *Jane* makes spasmodic gestures at is a peculiar combination of the two strands: nudge-nudge seaside-postcard smut crossed with kidnap and car chases. More interestingly still, it does so in a variety of locations ignored by the exclusive focus of more serious and substantial films on the area demarcated by the piers and seafront. Not only do we get to see Brighton station (both inside and out); there's also footage of Rottingdean (the Tudor Close Hotel, evidently in decline from its Bette Davis-hosting glory days of the 1930s), the Waterhall Mill on Mill Road (the criminals' hideout!), and the roads and lanes surrounding Devil's Dyke.

So what are the elements that still make *The Adventures of Jane* worth watching sixty years on? One of them has to be the character of Jane herself. Devised and drawn by Norman Pett (who can be seen working on a highly-contrived view of 'Jane in the Navy' beneath the film's opening titles), *Jane's Journal – Or the Diary of a Bright Young Thing* ran in the *Daily Mirror* from 1932 to 1959, reaching a peak of popularity during the war years. Churchill was said to have described Jane as 'Britain's Secret Weapon'; the young Lew Grade certainly had a hand in her being voted 'Britain's Perfect Girl', and signed Christabel Leighton-Porter (the model for the cartoon from the late 1930s on) as a semi-nude touring attraction. This is the rather raffish (by 1949 standards) milieu in which the Jane of the film is seen to earn her living. As a result, we're offered backstage glimpses of hard-drinking 'theatricals' (including a drag artiste) presented as a self-contained culture, an alternative to the conformity of the postwar years. Everyone in the film seems to take for granted Jane's fame, independence (not least from lecherous men) and frequent states of undress: in one of the most bizarre sequences, she's even installed as the evidently-overqualified prizegiver in a Rottingdean glamour contest. The slogan on the film's poster (*Now On The Screen In Person!*) emphasised this conflation of strip cartoon with reality, perhaps reflecting the willingness with which British servicemen had bought into the idea that a cartoon woman could be both sexually desirable and blithely matter-of-fact. However, although UK cinema attendances were at their peak in the late 1940s, the popularity of Jane was already on the slide by 1949, and there's a sense of desperation about the attempt to extend the franchise to films. Significantly, Brighton Studios made no effort at a follow-up, and the charming but wooden Mrs Leighton-Porter retired a few years later for a life of domesticity and Conservative Association fundraising in Horsham.

If Jane is perfectly 'of her time', so too are the film's villains. We're presented with a gang adopting the postures and (in at least one embarrassing case) attempting the accents of American hoodlums; at the same time, they manage to be utterly incompetent in implementing both their 'Bulawayo Diamond' scam and their subsequent kidnap of Jane. (She manages to deploy her trusty dachshund, Fritz, to send a note requesting help – from Mill Road via Devil's Dyke to Rottingdean! – and then proceeds to bombard the kidnappers with china from a handily-placed Welsh dresser.) At a time when films like *Brighton Rock*, *They Made Me a Fugitive* and the notorious *No Orchids for Miss Blandish* had sensitised British audiences to the genuinely violent underbelly of organised crime, *The Adventures of Jane* must have seemed like light relief from a gentler age. Only at one startling moment does the threat of real violence intrude: when 'The Boss' (an elderly gentleman who has previously seemed the epitome of leering but harmless decrepitude) suddenly pulls a gun on Ruby (the film's only other woman of any substance or rationale for existing), demanding her bracelet and warning her to 'keep your trap shut!' By the end of the film, however, even this allegedly dangerous criminal mastermind is reduced to having his stalled car restarted by the AA during an inept getaway attempt; comic decorum is thereby restored.

Which brings us to the climactic car chase. This sequence is unusual for British films of the period, both in its length and elaboration; three cars are involved, all intersecting with other vehicles and (at one point) a full-scale foxhunt. However, any sense of tension – even in the throwing-out of Jane down a steep embankment – is vitiated by camera overcranking which speeds the action up to cartoonish levels, redeemed only by a moment of near-Eisensteinian montage when two of the cars eventually collide. (As for the plot contrivance which has the miraculously unruffled Jane catching the diamond bracelet which 'the Boss' throws from his car in an effort to escape eventual detection, the less said the better.) However, the sequence remains topographically fascinating as an illustration of the largely deserted and unspoilt terrain around Devil's Dyke in the immediate postwar era.

Last and best of all: *The Adventures of Jane* remains (with the exception of *Quadrophenia* and *A Handful of Dust*) the only Brighton-based film to actually include a Brighton cinema as a backdrop for its action. And while *Quadrophenia* shows only brief glimpses of the old ABC (anachronistically playing Warren Beatty's *Heaven Can Wait* during an alleged bank holiday in 1964!) and *A Handful of Dust* uses just the entrance of the Duke of York's (dressed up as a generic cinema), *Jane* offers us both the exterior and part of the interior of the old Gaiety on Lewes Road. While the film contrives to recast the Gaiety as an out-of-Brighton 'variety theatre' (Jane is afterwards seen to travel to the 'Grand Theatre, Brighton' by train, and thence to Rottingdean by car), there's no mistaking its distinctive art deco frontage – complete with unlit neon tubing – in the opening scenes. It remains one of the ironies of Brighton film history that this quintessential 1930s picture palace later had its name changed to the Vogue, ending up hosting 'adult entertainment' of a considerably more explicit and sleazy nature than the 'Jane & Fritz' variety act advertised by the billboard in 'Adventures'. Many of us can still remember the sad sight of its corrugated-iron-fronted shell after its eventual closure in 1979, before it disappeared forever beneath what is still known as the Vogue Gyratory. Given that many in Brighton still view this triumph of ill-conceived and frankly dangerous road layout as the final revenge of East Sussex planners on a soon-to-be-independent Brighton, it seems doubly sad that the name imposed by them should have stuck. In memory of both Jane (whose cartoon surname, though unmentioned in the film, was Gay) and the once-splendid venue in which she 'played', would it not be much more appropriate to rename it the Gaiety Gyratory? Much more Brighton, too …

'I remember going to the Gaiety in the Lewes Road, which was the dirty cinema in those days, you didn't go to the Gaiety unless you wanted to see a dirty film. And they'd got *Victim* – a Dirk Bogarde film. And I remember being very moved by it, it touched nerves within me, you know? I mean, I didn't comprehend the blackmail thing because it had never happened to me but I remember the young boy being infatuated with the older man and I remember the shock of the garage door coming down and it had got 'queer' written on it. — **George, *Daring Hearts*, 1992. QueenSpark Books**

I think the first film I sneaked into was when I was at school, I was about fifteen – I suppose. It was *Only Two Can Play* (1962) with Peter Sellers and Mai Zetterling. And that was at the Ace or the Gaiety which is along Lewes Road. It is where the Sainsbury's is (on the Lewes Road). I think someone said it was haunted! But it was very funny. It had no atmosphere as cinema. You could imagine it being haunted because it was very dark. There was Coxes' pill factory and then there was a road that used to go up to Hollingdean. I think it was near the gyratory system, on that corner. So it must have been not far from Coxes'. But it was a horrible place. The last film I saw there in the late 1960s was *Easy Rider*, which was really a sad film actually. Well I think it struggled on – it was the Gaiety and then it became the Ace and then people stopped going there. It was all about the same time the Astoria packed up. – **Geraldine Curran**

I worked at the Vogue as a projectionist from 1974 until its closure. It was owned at that time by the Classic Cinema Group which also ran the Classic cinema in Western Road, now Waitrose where I also worked. I learnt my trade at the cinema, and am currently at the Duke of York's cinema in Preston Circus. – **Jimmy Anderson**

ASTORIA

(1933–1977)

FIRST FILM SCREENED

The Private Life of Henry VIII by Alexander Korda, in 1933.

DID YOU KNOW?

The Astoria Moving Picture Trust was formed by local cinema experts, Colin Dibley, Matthew May, and Brighton architect Nimrod Ping, who managed to get the building Grade II listed in November 2000; the listing makes special mention of the 'proscenium frieze work of unusual quality', and the 'unusual French art deco style' built to show that a south-coast location could 'match the West End in sophistication'.

DUSASHENKA

DESPITE HAVING BEEN CLOSED TO THE PUBLIC FOR more than ten years, and not having screened a movie in over thirty, the Astoria remains one of Brighton's most fondly remembered cinemas. Opened in the teeth of economic depression in December 1933 its somewhat bland stone faced exterior belied the elaborate art deco delights within. This was a picture palace designed to combine luxury with modernity. A cinema organ could be mechanically raised through a stage trapdoor at the start of each performance. The 1823-seat capacity made its opening (with full civic ceremony, and a screening of Korda's unashamedly decadent *The Private Life of Henry VIII*) a major event – despite the existence of fourteen other cinemas in central Brighton already.

Its prominent position at the hub of Brighton's tramway system on the Level ensured that it drew large audiences from a wide area despite being the ABC chain's second cinema in the town.

Architect EA Stone, who went on to build the Warner Leicester Square, created a gold-and-rose colour scheme, with art deco designs around the stage and in the foyer and stairs. The striking 150 foot-long facade along Gloucester Place was spectacularly lit up at night to complement the fountains along Victoria Gardens. The Astoria was one of the first cinemas outside London to have a licensed bar, and huge first-floor windows looked out from luxurious tea-rooms and a restaurant. The 20 foot-deep stage, four dressing rooms and stage door allowed for full band shows, and variety stars were to include Arthur Askey, Dickie Valentine, Alma Cogan and Frankie Vaughan.

After the war the art-deco interior was partly concealed, including the nude art-deco goddesses reclining above the proscenium arch. Variety shows ended and the organ was removed (though it may still exist, and much of the equipment for raising it remains).

Site of the Astoria Cinema, circa 1932

THE ROYAL PAVILION AND MUSEUMS, BRIGHTON & HOVE

Exterior of the Astoria
Cinema, circa 1933

The Astoria was notable not only for its decor, but
also for its record of technical innovation, particularly
after TV viewing began to affect cinema attendance in the
1950s. Facilities included deaf aids and a huge illuminated
Compton 3 manual organ. It was the only Brighton cinema
to succeed with the 3D gimmick in 1953 (running *House of
Wax* for four consecutive weeks), it was one of the first to be
adapted for CinemaScope in 1954; and was, for some time,
the only cinema in Sussex equipped to screen the 70mm
blockbusters of the late 1950s. Widescreen kept the crowds
coming, with huge runs of up to 56 weeks for blockbusters
like *South Pacific, Gigi, Oklahoma, Doctor Zhivago, 2001*, and
in 'Sensurround,' *The Towering Inferno*.

Throughout its forty-four year life as a cinema, the
Astoria is probably best remembered for its extended runs
of family oriented fare. The last film ever screened there,
before movies gave way to the unstoppable tide of bingo in
1977 – which continued until 1997 when the then-owner Gala
opened a purpose-built bingo hall in Eastern Road – was the

*We are the boys and
girls from Brighton,
members of the ABC,*

*And every Saturday
we line up, to see
the films we love and
shout aloud with glee.*

*We are are the boys and
girls from Brighton, what
a happy band are we-ee.*

*We're are all pals together,
we're members of the ABC.*

The tune was a
Sousa March, I think.
Another song was:
*There's a worm at the
bottom of the garden
whose name is Wiggly Woo.*

I will now go hide
and hope that
my mates are not
reading this! Happy
days. – Patrick Collins

Foyer of the Astoria
Cinema, circa 1955

Streisand / Kristofferson remake of *A Star is Born*. Above all, its fortunes seem to be tied up with that ultimate box-office draw, *Gone with the Wind*, which made its Brighton debut there in 1940, before returning for further long runs in 1942, 1968-69 and 1975. Given that the Astoria is once more for sale at the time of writing, it would make a fairy-tale ending if some charitable soul (a lottery winner, perhaps) could restore it to its former glory and reopen with a further revival of Scarlett and Rhett. Any takers?

Like so many other kids in the pre-TV age I went there [The Astoria] every Saturday morning between about 1957 and 1963 for the wonderful ABC Minors children's film shows. The shows commenced with a sing-along to various pub standards – *My Old Man Said Follow The Van*, etc. – accompanied by bouncing-ball prompt on screen. This invariably culminated with *We Are The ABC Minors* sung to the tune of a well-known military march whose title escapes me. – **Len Liechti**

My recollections date from the late 1940s. The march tune was *Blaze Away*, I think by W. Rimmer and dated from the First World War. – **Raymond (Dickie) Bird**

DUSASHENKA

DUSASHENKA

Interior of the Astoria
Cinema, circa 1955

I think I must have marched miles in and behind bands playing it and always sang the same old words. Ain't it strange the things that stick in your mind over the years? Good old times in the 1940s but better still when the rationing finished. – **Patrick Collins**

There then followed a cartoon – *Bugs Bunny, Tom and Jerry*, etc. – a short Pathé Pictorial documentary and a serial. The latter were the classic pre-war black-and-white cliffhangers and I particularly recall *Zorro, Batman* (pre-Robin) and *Flash Gordon*. After the interval there came a feature film, often in monochrome but occasionally, and excitingly, in colour. Examples were *The Legion's Last Patrol* with Alan Ladd, *The Alamo* with John Wayne and the various *Sinbad* adventures.

The whole programme started at 9am and finished at midday. Entrance was sixpence for the stalls and ninepence for the circle (old money, of course). My mother would give me a shilling (5 pence) to pay for entrance (6d), a Lyon's ice lolly (3d) and bus fare on the 26 trolley between St Saviour's and St Peter's (three-halfpence each way). Sometimes I'd

THE ROYAL PAVILION AND MUSEUMS, BRIGHTON & HOVE

Organist at the
Astoria, 1935

walk and use the saved bus fares to pay for admission to the circle. The kids in the circle would often drop their ice-lolly sticks and other sticky objects on the kids below in the stalls, and I must admit to occasionally succumbing to the temptation to do the same. – **Len Liechti**

Rather than employ an entire staff of adults, the manager got some of the older children to act as monitors and then gave them free entry. I was a monitor there and recall having to give out picture cards to the smaller children attending. The aim was to get them to collect entire sets by coming back week after week. When they had a full set, they got a badge. As monitors we always ensured we got full sets of the cards and the badges. I've still got some tucked away in a drawer somewhere. While the kids were at the Saturday morning cinema, busy mums had to dash from shop to shop in London Road to get the weekend groceries. No supermarkets in those days.

The mothers often went to Bellmans, where the sales

ROYAL CIRCLE
BALCONY
CIRCLE SEATS 32·29
THIS WAY PLEASE

DUSASHENKA

The Astoria foyer, 1935

assistants put all money tendered into a catapult system and shot it across the ceiling on wire to the cashier's desk. After that they were off to Sydney Street, where butchers wearing bloodstained aprons and boaters often stood in the road outside their shops discounting their meat. Each joint had a little wire skewer in it, and at the end of the day you could often get two joints for the price of one. – **Roy Grant**

I had to do the family chores so I didn't get to see Saturday morning films. I wasn't keen on those anyway because if you couldn't afford to go the following week you'd miss what was going on. And I think it was very noisy with screams and shouts, from the children. Mind you, saying that, I used to send my own children to Saturday morning pictures at the Astoria. But that was to get rid of them for a couple of hours. – **Diana Meeten**

[The Astoria] was a fabulous cinema, on the Steine by St Peter's Church, that had terrific character. I think the

Astoria used to have CinemaScope – I saw *Dr Zhivago* there.
The last film I saw there was *The Exorcist*. Well I had to come
out because I felt violently sick , I actually felt faint … so
I never saw all of it … it wasn't until about 10 years ago
I actually saw all of it. My nephew got it on video and it's
still horrific, even now. – **Geraldine Curran**

The kids in East Brighton came from very poor
backgrounds – cinema-going was there, but there was a
kind of mental divide – people didn't travel very far, so
going to the town – crossing the London Road – was a
huge mental step. So if there was a big blockbuster film on
at the Astoria – it tended to have long-run films on, like
West Side Story (1961) for three or four months at a time,
with CinemaScope and stereophonic sound and all the rest
of it – that would be a big special treat, to go and see the
new blockbuster film. – **Bryan Moody**

My other abiding memory of the Astoria was going to see
2001: a Space Odyssey on its first release in 1968, shortly
before I left for university in Bath. This brilliant psychedelic
movie on the huge screen, the soundtrack booming through
the massive speakers, left an impression on me that has
never faded, and it remains my favourite film to this day.
I recall walking home still trying to fathom out what the
ending was about. – **Len Liechti**

The Astoria
exterior, 2009

HENRY BRUCE

DAVE HUGGINS

THE
BIG SCREEN

SOME DAYS IN THE LIFE OF DAVE HUGGINS

ALTHOUGH LOGIE BAIRD WAS WELL INTO INVENTING television in the 1930s, it was still some 20 years away for the masses. In 1938 a very flickery, early model was installed at the Devil's Dyke Hotel, about five miles outside Brighton. From what I had heard, the programmes were even worse than today's.

I walked with Neville, my best pal, to the Dyke to see their new wonder. We asked the manager if we could take a look. The second word of his answer was 'off'. Never mind the lack of television – my family couldn't even afford a wireless. That's why going to the pictures was so important to us. All us kids used to read about the forthcoming attractions in the *Argus*, our local paper. Every cinema displayed still photographs of the film outside. It took us a long time to make up our minds which films to see. Our pocket money was too hard-won to waste on boring films.

Part-time work, including paper rounds and helping the greengrocer, fuelled the delight of those hours spent in semi-darkness with that huge coned beam of light overhead weaving adventures that delighted my young eyes. The Western sagas, such as *Drums along the Mohawk*, and tales of the empire – *Gunga Din*, *The Drum* and *Lives of Bengal Lancers* were my favourites.

My mum only applied a few rules when it came to cinema: never dishonestly slip in through the side door, and never, on pain of death, ask a man to take you in to an 'A' film. Films were categorised as H for horror, for over eighteens only; A was for over sixteens or those accompanied by an adult, and U denoted universal viewing, which meant everyone could see it.

One film etched in my memory depicted God as a black man. He had a wonderful voice and certainly got my vote for God. During the film a man in the audience jumped up and shouted 'Blasphemy!' Somebody else implied he should go forth and urinate. I was fascinated.

A wonderful opportunity presented itself to us youngsters at Hove's Lido Cinema – the Saturday morning Mickey Mouse Club. Membership was free and we were all presented with a card and a badge. The performance began with the club song, shown on the screen with a little ball dancing over the words to remind us:

Hi-de-hi, ho-de-ho, take your breath and sing / Hi-de-hi, ho-de-ho, let the password ring / We will do for Mickey Mouse our good deeds in Mickey's house / Mick gives us lots of fun. Cheer, for the party's begun.

The song was followed by a cowboy film or similar – a couple of cartoons and part of a serial depicting heroes such as Buck Rogers, or Flash Gordon defeating creatures from another galaxy. He was always left dangling by the skin of his teeth as a voice boomed: 'Is this the end of Flash Gordon?' All that wonderful excitement for threepence.

I think the good deeds referred to were: no fighting, no shooting air pistols at the screen to help Flash, and no peeing under the seat rather than miss the crucial bit of the serial. If the film broke down, we'd go crazy – shouting, booing, throwing apple cores and orange peel and chanting the old favourite, "Why are we waiting?" We wouldn't stop until the film had come back on.

It all went off the boil for me when it came to the children's Christmas party in 1938. Admission was by club card only. Following a Saturday morning roughhouse, Mum had boiled my bloodstained shirt with the club card in the breast pocket. I went to the Lido manager and explained what had happened, leaving out the bit about the fight. He looked at me and said, 'You are a naughty Mickey.' 'What a tosser,' I thought – and never returned.

Soon after, wonderful news spread through our area like wildfire. 'Have you heard about Dave Huggins? His mother's got a job as a cook at the Lido café. She gets a complimentary ticket for Dave every week. Lucky bugger!'

I shall never forget my first visit. My mum' s shift started at 6 PM. We went by bus, getting off at Hove station. The Lido was reputed to be the country's biggest single-storey cinema. I was introduced to a gorgeous little usherette who took me to the best seat in the house. The film started. Then another lovely girl approached me with a display case hanging by a strap from her shoulder. It contained sweets and chocolates. She came straight to me and passed me a bar of chocolate. She patted me on the cheek and disappeared like a heavenly vision. This can't get any better, I thought. But it did. During the interval, another lovely woman appeared and thrust a huge tub of ice cream into my sticky paws. I had obviously died and gone to heaven. At the end of the film, I was shown through a door into the Lido's kitchen. My mum had a big plate of egg and chips waiting for me. My cup runneth over! Well, certainly my stomach did. I felt very seedy on my way home.

Was my future in the free cinema assured? No – I was never taken again. Had I transgressed in some way? Broken some important rule? No, nothing like that, my mother explained. The chocolate and ice cream girls worked at the Lido for very small wages plus commission. It took a long time to earn the money back on any stock given away. They wouldn't listen to Mum when she asked them not to do it. So she did the only other thing possible – kept the freeloader away. I was horrified and bitterly disappointed at the time, but later in life realised just how much my mum cared about others.

Seeing films was not the only enjoyment we experienced through cinema. We would base our games on the adventures we had seen on the screen. I remember swinging on bits of clothesline from trees in the park, trying to imitate Tarzan's call. We would dress up in Dad's trilby with black stockings over our faces, making the Z-shaped mark of Zorro with a wooden sword over anything that showed scratches. Sometimes we rushed about slapping our own backsides as if we were horses, with our hands in the shape of guns. 'Bang, bang. You're dead,' we yelled. And became extremely annoyed if the person we shouted at refused to die. One of my pals acted out a death scene so well by grasping his chest that he fell from the branch of a tree onto a pile of grass cuttings. Unfortunately, they were covering up the roller. He broke his collarbone. If pictures were said to be 'make-believe', we certainly added our own imaginations.

MARTIN PAYNE

DUKE OF YORK'S
PICTUREHOUSE

(1910–PRESENT)

FIRST FILM SCREENED

Byways of Brighton by pioneer Hove film-maker
George Albert Smith who worked from a studio in
St Ann's Well Gardens and later Wilbury Villas.

DID YOU KNOW?

It was considered the height of luxury during its
early years and its famous advertising slogan was
'Bring her to the Duke's, it is fit for a Duchess'.

The iconic black and white striped cancan legs that protrude
from the cinema roof first appeared in 1991. The then owner,
Bill Heine, had them made for another cinema he owned
in Oxford called *Not* the Moulin Rouge. The legs are now
an integral part of the Duke of York's advertising logo.

SITUATED AT PRESTON CIRCUS, TO THE NORTH OF the city, the Duke of York's cinema first opened its doors on 22 September, 1910. This makes it by far the oldest cinema in town but also gives it the distinction of being the oldest cinema in the country that is still operating.

Previous page: View east of front of the Duke of York's circa 1910

Its official opening was presided over by the Mayor of Brighton, Charles Thomas-Stanford. As the cinema predates the advent of the feature film the opening programme would likely have consisted of several short films, one of which was called *Byways of Brighton* by local film pioneer George Albert Smith. It was built on the site of the old Amber Ale Brewery and a wall from that building still forms the rear part of the auditorium.

The cinema's first owner was Violet Melnotte-Wyatt who also, with her husband, owned the Duke of York's theatre in London's West End from which it takes its name.

Originally it had seating for 800 people but continuous remodelling of the interior over the years means it seats a little over 300 now. Also, one of its original two boxes still remains on the balcony. Despite all the remodelling it has only ever had one screen.

The Duke of York's, 2009

The Duke of York's became a members-only art house cinema in 1981 but this is no longer the case; it is now open to the general public also. Its programme of cult, foreign language and mainstream films, late night and Kids' Club screenings, monthly live music gigs, film quiz and special events, such as Britain's biggest Eurovision Song Party, has secured it a devoted audience, one just as likely to buy coffee and cake to enjoy during the film as popcorn. It also has the city's only auditorium that is licensed for the consumption of alcohol.

Currently owned by City Screen Limited, the Duke of York's Picturehouse has been a Grade II listed building since 1994. It will be celebrating its centenary in 2010.

HENRY BRUCE

HENRY BRUCE

The Duke of York's
by night, 2009

A Saturday morning at the Duke of York's Cinema was our special treat for the previous week's good behaviour when my two sisters and I were young. I remember the excitement of being somewhere on our own, without grown-ups watching our every move. The decision of where we were to sit often caused arguments between us ... I remember the hard seats, which I found very uncomfortable and the material with which they were covered was itchy and irritated my legs. In our innocence, we wondered why there were double seats in the back row. We have since discovered the reason! I always wanted to sit in the back row because invariably, wherever we sat, the people in front of us were blessed with either big heads or had stiff "Eiffel Tower" hairstyles, and if there were no people directly behind us, we could just sit on the seats unopened, which made us higher. – **Susie Mehmed,** *On the Writing Trail: Short Stories by QueenSpark Writers.* QueenSpark Books, 1999

During the war we used to go there because we couldn't afford heating and electricity so we thought we'd go there for three hours before we went to bed and keep warm. So we used to use the Duke of York's in Preston Circus, next door to the old fire station.

...it was only seven old pennies to get in and then as we got more affluent we went up to the ten pence seats and then I think it went up to one and thruppence after that, and that was up in the balcony ... Mum used to give us a ten shilling note because she hadn't got any change for the three of us to go and if there was a queue we used to go in the expensive seats and give her what was left.

I remember going to the Duke of York's one day, on my own on a Saturday afternoon, because I got pocket money for doing my grandma's shopping, so I was able to go in the afternoon and I was probably sixteen and this soldier tried to chat me up. – **Diana Meeten**

I still remember eating chips on the way up New England Hill after our very first film in about 1954 – *Shane* with Alan Ladd at the Duke of York's. The tingle of excitement as the

The Duke of York's, 1920

little boy looked under the saloon doors at
the end of the film; I can still conjure. I can
only compare that with the battle scenes in
Olivier's *Henry V* at the Continentale (Kemp
Town) in a primary school trip and *The
Gun* at the Regent, I think, although that
was a close-run thing with *The Admirable
Crichton* at the Odeon near Hove Station.
(The Odeon was later replaced by social
security offices, car showrooms, Norman's
supermarket and now Hove General Post

Postcard showing
George Albert Smith's
studio in St Ann's Well
Gardens, date unknown

Office sorting office). The cartoons and newsreels in North
Street did not have the same impact, although *Snow White*
at the Embassy is still fresh. – **Andy Steer, Brighton Boy:
A Fifties Childhood. 1994. QueenSpark Books**

I used to like being taken to the Duke of York's Cinema
nearby. I believe this was my first cinema. The films were
shown in black and white, with no sound, only a piano being
played. Laurel and Hardy and Charlie Chaplin films were my
favourites and still make me laugh today. Charles Laughton
left a vivid impression on me when I saw him in the film
Jamaica Inn, which in parts, I found rather frightening.
When I saw *Snow White and the Seven Dwarfs*, which was
in colour, I was very frightened of the witch. I believe
even when it was shown in later years some children
were frightened of the witch and this part of the film was
changed. When Charlie Chaplin's talking film *Modern Times*
was to be shown, cinemas had to have new equipment
installed to be able to hear and see this film, which everyone
thought was marvellous. A child star, named Shirley Temple,
became my favourite child actress and I used to plead to be
taken to see all her films. – **Barbara Chapman Boxing Day Baby.
1994. QueenSpark Books**

More cinemas opened, and whereas we used to go to the
Duke of York's (which is still operating at Preston Circus)
now there was a choice. As it had become big business in
America, we also had more films showing here (in black and
white, of course). After films like *The Perils of Pauline*, which
showed the action, followed by the caption, these films were
much more exciting as they were "talkies", where the actors'

HENRY BRUCE

The black and white striped can-can legs first appeared in 1991 and are now an integral part of the Duke of York's advertising logo

voices were heard. *The Perils of Pauline* had been exciting at the time, mainly because it was a serial which ended with the heroine in some cliff hanging situation, like being tied to a railway line with a train coming ever nearer. Suddenly the caption would read, "Will the hero reach Pauline in time? Find out next week." – **Marjorie Batchelor, *A Life Behind Bars*. 1999. QueenSpark Books**

The Dome and Pavilion became hospitals for wounded Indians. We used to go down and talked to them through the railings with nods and smiles, sometimes a whole charabanc of them would be taken to the Duke of York's in Preston Circus. The Germans were using poisoned gas and a lot of men suffered damage to their lungs. – *Blighty Brighton*. **1994. QueenSpark Books**

I like sitting at the back or in the middle and I like the Duke of York's cinema. I love adverts and I loved the film *Wall-E*. A film that made me cry was *ET*. I *hate* love films. A horrid film I saw was *Indiana Jones and Raiders of the Lost Ark*. The soldiers' faces melt in it. I really want to see a zombie film. My mum shows funny Spanish films at the Jubilee library. I like films in English and Spanish. I love going to the cinema! – **Stani, seven**

The last film I saw at the cinema was *Wild Child*. It is my second favourite film, and I went with my mum and my best friend Lydia. I went to see it at the end of the school holidays. My favourite part was when Poppy went shopping with all her friends and they turned all the shabby clothes into brilliant glamorous dresses. Me and Lydia loved it! I usually go to the Duke of York's. I go there practically every Saturday morning with my dad at ten o'clock for Kids' Club and for the drawing competition. I've won twice! There's also a raffle. I haven't won that yet. – **Scout, ten**

The Duke of York's I used to go to as a child – I certainly remember watching *Zulu* (1964) there – they used to run continuous performances, and they didn't throw you out – you could come in in the middle of a film and watch it through, so you could see the end first. – **John (former projectionist)**

MARTIN PAYNE

THE
ELECTRIC
BIOSCOPE AND BEYOND

(1909–1979)

LAST FILM SCREENED ON THIS SITE

Either *The Warriors* or *The Spaceman and King Arthur*,
when the cinema was operating as the Classic.

DID YOU KNOW?

Where Waitrose supermarket now stands on
Western Road once stood a cinema that went through
more name changes than perhaps any other in the City.

THE ROYAL PAVILION AND MUSEUMS, BRIGHTON & HOVE

THERE IS SOME CONFUSION ABOUT THE DATE THE cinema opened and its first name. It either opened in January 1907 as the Electric Theatre or in January 1909 as the Electric Bioscope. Either way, it soon got renamed the Queen's Electric Theatre (1910-1915). Subsequent names included the Queen's Picture Theatre (1915-1919), Picturedrome (1919-1922), Scala Cinema (1922-1932), Regal Cinema (1932-1936) and Curzon Kinema, which remained its name from 1936 through to 1975. Its final incarnation was as the Classic Cinema, which became its name in July 1975 until it closed in the Autumn of 1979.

Originally only the size of a small shop, seating about fifty people, the boom in cinema-going soon enabled it to expand its premises to seat 250 and include an orchestra pit. This was at the time when silent films were still given a live soundtrack. It is a matter of record that it resisted the introduction of 'talking pictures' for a while.

The Scala Cinema,
Western Road, 1930

By the late 1930s, as the Curzon, it had a capacity for an audience of over 650, while forty years later, as the Classic, the number of seats is recorded as 597. Its last screening was of the film *The Warriors* before its doors were finally closed, over seventy years after they had first opened. It was sold to the John Lewis Partnership.

THE ROYAL PAVILION AND MUSEUMS, BRIGHTON & HOVE

The Curzon Kinema,
Western Road
circa 1936

'I remember sitting in Brighton's Curzon cinema for more than seven hours, watching Errol Flynn lead the Light Brigade to glory. In those days films were shown continuously and you could stay as long as you liked – or dared. – **Dave Huggins**

In about 1937 my Grandma would take me to the Curzon or the Tiv (the Tivoli along the road at 1 Western Road, Hove). She was short-sighted and we sat in the sixpenny seats, front row, and got a neck-ache! In 1948 my boyfriend and I found we didn't have enough money to buy tickets at the Tiv, so he went down the queue and sold some postage stamps: new ones not licked! – **June**

I worked at the Vogue as a projectionist from 1974 until its closure. It was owned at that time by the Classic Cinema Group, which also ran the Classic cinema in Western Road, now Waitrose, where I also worked. I learnt my trade at the cinema, and am currently at the Duke of York's cinema in Preston Circus. – **Jimmy Anderson**

PAUL BLAND

The Classic (formerly Curzon) in the early 1970s

AMY RILEY

—————

THE
GRANADA

(1933–1974)

FIRST FILM SCREENED
The Kiss Before The Mirror and *The Hawleys Of High Street.*

DID YOU KNOW?
Along with the Granada (Dover), the Granada (Hove) ran independently from the Granada chain, until the freeholds for both were purchased by the ABC cinema chain in 1935. Neither cinema was given the ABC name until years later, in May 1965.

T HE GRANADA CINEMA ON PORTLAND ROAD IS ONE of those well-loved places that has brought out residents to fight for its survival not just once, but twice. Located in the heart of a busy residential area, the cinema functioned for forty years as a movie theatre, then again as a bingo hall.

It opened its doors on 17 July 1933 with screenings of *The Kiss Before the Mirror* and *The Hawleys of High Street*. The cinema was owned by Granada (Dover) Ltd, but was then bought by the ABC company who also owned The Savoy on East Street and Astoria on Gloucester Place.

The 1,638-seat cinema boasted a Compton cinema organ, a forty-five-foot proscenium and twenty-five-foot deep stage, and the complex also ran a café and sun terrace. The cinema acquired a Westrex sound system in 1948 and remained well-used until April 1974, when the cinema's closure was proposed. This did not go down well.

For two months, local people demonstrated and signed petitions to keep the Granada open.

The building was turned into a Lucky Seven bingo hall by Ladbrokes. The bingo hall stayed open for another thirty years, before shutting in 2003.

As the ABC in 1965

DUSASHENKA

Since 2003, the old cinema has been the centre of another dramatic legal battle. Residents spent two years fighting developers and the Brighton & Hove City Council to save the building from demolition, as plans were under way to transform the site into a multi-storey block of flats. The residents won, but plans to develop the building into a multi-function recreational and community facility are still on hold. From its original grand art-deco state to the modified state as a garish Gala bingo hall, the cinema now sits empty today.

The Granada, that was a very classy cinema in Portland Road, which is derelict now … it was a lovely cinema, fantastic. The last thing I saw there was probably *Gone with the Wind* which they re-released in the 1970s and I think I saw *Midnight Cowboy* there too. They had this art deco – rich carpets and the lighting. It was all very … it wasn't like a fleapit … the Rothbury was a sort of fleapit. – **Geraldine Curran**

The building in 2009

HENRY BRUCE

HENRY BRUCE

MARTIN PAYNE

HOORAY FOR
HOLLYWOOD

George Albert Smith's studio in St Ann's Well Gardens, Hove in 1902, with the rooftop set for the film *Mary Jane's Mishap*.

DID YOU KNOW?

Smith was one of the pioneers of Victorian cinema. He leased St Ann's Well Gardens in 1892 where he started his film making. In 1897 he acquired his first camera and by the end of the year he had already made thirty-one films.

B RIGHTON & HOVE HAS A LONG, ILLUSTRIOUS HISTORY of filmmaking and any movie buff with stamina, and a Saver bus ticket, could spend an enjoyable day travelling the length and breadth of the city tracing the history of its films and lost cinemas. Of course those with less time and energy can just as easily take a virtual tour, and the best place to start, to quote Julie Andrews, is right at the very beginning.

As unlikely as it seems now, our city once rivalled Hollywood in terms of expertise and output, and it all began on 25 March 1896 when Brighton became the first town outside of London to host a public film exhibition in Britain. The programme consisted of a series of short films made by French brothers Auguste and Louis Lumière and the venue was the Pandora Gallery at 132 Kings Road. So successful were the shows, and such was the public demand for this new innovation, that a few months later on 1 July the Pandora, newly named the Victoria Hall, commenced regular screenings, thus becoming Brighton's first cinema. The Melrose restaurant now stands on the site, opposite the West Pier, where you can view a blue plaque commemorating its illustrious past.

The Victorian era saw a burst of activity in Brighton and Hove by several pioneers of the fledgling film industry who were eager to push forward the boundaries of this new art form. In fact, some of these men are credited with inventing techniques that to this day are an integral part of the language of filmmaking. Esmé Collings, William Friese-Greene, Alfred Darling, George Albert Smith, James Williamson, John Benett-Stanford, Charles Urban and Robert Paul all played their part and perhaps inevitably, given the size of the town, their histories are intertwined. Space here doesn't allow for details of all their achievements but, in keeping with the spirit of a whistle-stop tour, these few are worthy of a mention.

In 1896 Collings was operating as one of Britain's first filmmakers, out of his workshop at 120 Western Road. It seems fitting, given Brighton's reputation for seediness, that he also made a short

Early Biocam and accessories made by Alfred Darling

Charles Urban and an unidentified man pictured with a Bioscope camera mounted on a tripod (late 1890s / early 1900s)

film called *Woman Undressing* that is often credited as being the world's first 'blue' movie.

Darling was a skilled engineer who made film equipment for Smith and Collings. He started his business from his bedroom at 47 Chester Terrace, Brighton and Darling & Sons Engineering still trades to this day near Moulsecoomb Station.

Smith was a leaseholder of St Ann's Well Gardens in Hove. In 1897 he opened a film laboratory in the garden's pump house. By 1910 he'd acquired a studio close to Hove station where he continued to make films using a two colour additive process called 'Kinemacolor', which he helped develop. The word 'Kinemacolor' can still be read on the side of a building on the site. Smith retired to 18 Chanctonbury Road, Hove where a blue plaque marks his achievements.

Williamson started out with a chemist shop at 144 Church Road, Hove and his customers included Collings, Darling and Smith who all came to buy chemicals for developing their films. His interest was piqued and he began making films in 1898, later building a film studio in his garden at 55 Western Road, Hove.

In 1907 Friese-Greene, who had briefly been in partnership with Collings, opened a film laboratory at 20 Middle Street, Brighton, where a blue plaque credits him with being 'the inventor of cinematography'. His real interest, however, lay in developing his own colour film process, 'Biocolour', in direct competition with 'Kinemacolor', which he eventually put out of business.

A good place to investigate these pioneers, and fully appreciate their legacy, is at Hove Museum & Art Gallery, 19 New Church Road, Hove. Here you will find detailed

James Williamson

Williamson's Chemists, 144 Church Road, Hove

A ESMÉ COLLINGS

BRIGHTON

69 Western Road.

W

LONDON STUDIO

121 New Bond Street.

W

Sign for Esmé
Collings' studio

Hove Museum has a
wonderful interactive
display detailing over
forty former cinema
sites. Alternatively you
can read about some
of them online at www.
mybrightonandhove.org.uk

Ray Allister's book,
*Friese-Greene: Close-up
of an Inventor* (London:
Marsland, 1948)

biographies put into a historical context, amid showcases crammed with early filmmaking equipment. Most impressively though, you can watch continuous performances of a number of their films. It's astonishing to think that some of these black and white shorts are 108 years old and that you are witnessing the birth of the movie industry.

Away from the 'Who's Who?' and the 'What?' and 'When?' of the technical stuff you might like to divert yourself by (flea) pit stops around town to view the buildings and sites where the city's old cinemas once stood.

In the 1940s, the heyday of film-going in this country, there were twenty-four cinemas in Brighton and Hove, although many others came and went both before and after that decade. The tell-tale shape of several can still be seen today, incorporated into their latest incarnations.

The Continentale in Sudeley Place, Kemp Town started life as a chapel, ended its cinematic career showing soft-porn and still survives as a sheltered housing development. Burger King on North Street, Brighton now resides where the Bijou Electric Theatre used to stand. The former Tivoli, latterly an amusement arcade, now stands empty at 1 Western Road, Hove. The Granada on Portland Road, Hove finished life as a bingo hall and is now derelict. The Rothbury, Franklin Road, Portslade now houses the Southern FM Radio studios.

Then there are the sites where picture houses used to stand, before the property developers moved in, and where you will now find more familiar names. Examples in Brighton include The Electric Bioscope, now Waitrose (Western Road), The Imperial Cinema, now Morrisons (St James's Street), and The Gem Electric Theatre, now The Woolwich Building Society (London Road).

Some, however, left us only their name. The Vogue (formerly The Gaiety) on Lewes Road was demolished to make way for the road system that now bears its name, the Vogue Gyratory, while others played a more influential role. The Regent, perhaps the grandest of all Brighton's former cinemas, used to stand on the site now occupied by Boots on North

Street. The local press called it 'A gorgeous temple of silent drama' and at its peak it could seat 3,000 people. Among its regular customers were two small boys, Roy and John Boulting, who took inspiration from these dramas played out before them and, in adult life, went on to produce and direct Graham Greene's *Brighton Rock* (1947). A plaque on the wall by the Queens Road entrance of Boots details the Regent's history.

It would be impossible to write about the history of cinemas here without making special mention of the Duke of York's cinema at Preston Circus, Brighton. It first opened its doors on 22 September 1910 and now has the distinction of being the oldest cinema showing films continuously in Britain.

The furthest our tour takes us is out to Shoreham beach. Filmmaker F L Lyndhurst was making movies on the site as early as 1912, and in 1915 he built a studio made of glass, appropriately named the Glasshouse Studio, in order to capitalise on the natural light the site offered because the studio had no electricity. The economic climate of the First World War closed production down but in 1920 producer Stanley Morgan bought the site and started making his own films, many starring his daughter Joan, and movie making thrived there until his company went out of business in 1929. It was Joan who unveiled a blue plaque to mark the centenary of cinema in 1996 on the site at King's Gap that is now occupied by a children's home.

No chapter about the history of cinema in Brighton and Hove is, of course, complete without a mention of some of the more, relatively, recent films that have used the city as a location. *Brighton Rock* (1947) and *Quadrophenia* (1979) may be the best remembered but there is a long list of others. Among them, *Genevieve* (1953), *Oh! What a Lovely War* (1969), *On a Clear Day You Can See Forever* (1970), *Carry On at Your Convenience* (1971), *Mona Lisa* (1986), *The End of the Affair* (1999) and *Wimbledon* (2004). There is a curious satisfaction to be had from watching these films now to see how the city has changed from decade to decade. Some

William Friese-Greene (1855–1921) moved to Brighton in 1905

would also admit to a thrill at tracing the footsteps of Barbra Streisand through the grounds of the Royal Pavilion, Kenneth Williams along Brighton Pier, or Ralph Fiennes and Julianne Moore under the arches on Madeira Drive.

The old town gives a good account of herself as the gracious hostess, and whatever it was that first attracted filmmakers to these parts, the light, the architecture, the atmosphere and the local expertise, obviously still act as a lure to this day. We may no longer rival Hollywood in terms of output, and we may not have tours of film stars' homes, but a trip around our city proves that our association with cinema and celluloid has been very influential and just as enduring.

FRANK FLOOD

THE
MYLES BYRNE
CINEMAS

CINESCENE & CONTINENTALE

LAST FILM SCREENED
The Ploughman's Lunch (1983) by Richard Eyre.

DID YOU KNOW?
As well as being a cinema owner, Myles Byrne (1919–1986)
also ran the theatre at the end of the Palace Pier.
His name appears on the front of one of Brighton & Hove's buses.

DUSASHENKA

MYLES BYRNE WAS EVIDENTLY THE SORT OF character who belongs in a good comic novel. At the same time as being an enthusiastically Thatcherite 'hang 'em and flog 'em' Conservative councillor and respectable owner of a chain of small cinemas and theatres along the south coast, he also managed to promote the cause of serious non-Hollywood film in Brighton over more than three decades – latterly by using the profits from screening low-rent European pornographic films at his one-time flagship, the Continentale in Kemptown, to subsidise 'art house' cinema at the Cinescene in North Street. His death in 1986 was undoubtedly the end of an era in Brighton cinema.

Before its 'Myles Byrne Film Centre' rebranding, the Cinescene had already gone through more name changes than any other cinema in the area. Older residents will undoubtedly remember it as the Prince's, although it had originally opened in 1911 as the splendidly-titled Bijou Electric Empire (and then as the Select Palace in 1918). It specialised in a mixture of newsreels and cartoons, all screened in a small and slightly lopsided auditorium that had once been a printing works. By the mid-1960s, the demise of cinema newsreels in the face of TV competition left the Princes in a financially shaky situation, and a further rebranding in 1966, as the Jacey, coincided with a switch to feature exhibitions of an 'erotic' and / or 'horrific' nature. This lasted for only three years before the British Film Institute bought the lease and relaunched the venue as the (now fondly-remembered) Brighton Film Theatre. For the next decade, this was undoubtedly the 'art house' venue that a town like Brighton needed, fulfilling much the same function as the Duke of York's did from the early 1980s onward; however, audiences remained disappointingly low, and the BFI withdrew their funding at the end of 1978.

Prince's cinema, North Street, Brighton, c1933
The large sign by the name indicates that it is showing 'Talkies'. A further sign above the door states that a Charlie Chaplin performance will be shown that day

THE ROYAL PAVILION AND MUSEUMS, BRIGHTON & HOVE

Which was where the estimable Mr Byrne stepped in: having pioneered often 'risqué', but equally often award-winning or challenging, European film screenings at the Continentale from the early 1950s onwards, he now purchased the BFT and relaunched it as the Cinescene while maintaining the 'art house' approach. Filmgoers of a certain age will have fond memories of the somewhat deaf and doddery old couple who ran the front-of-house operations for the next few years; alas, the quality of their tea and cakes was rarely equal to that of the films. The venue still lost money, however: indeed, the word around Brighton in 1982 was that it had only been kept going that year by the unexpected box office success of *The Draughtsman's Contract*, which played for six straight weeks despite the fact that the reels were supposed to have been delivered to the Duke of York's rather than the Cinescene, and that Byrne refused to either return them to the distributor or pay the rentals. A year later it finally closed, standing empty for half a decade before enduring the ultimate indignity of conversion into a 'film-themed' Burger King.

The cinema theme continues at the site of Cinescene inside Burger King and in their window display

The Continentale, which had been Byrne's first Brighton purchase in 1949, fared only slightly better, lurching on with a range of 'adult' features until its owner's death in 1986 and its subsequent conversion into flats. Perhaps unsurprisingly given its latter-day programming, first person recollections of the Continentale tend to be thin on the ground compared to those of other Brighton cinemas; but the present writer is surely not alone in regretting not having gone to experience the delights of such fare as *Eager Fingers*, *Eager Lips* and *Frank and I* at least once before another Brighton landmark closed its doors to the paying public for ever.

HENRY BRUCE

47

And of course there was the News Theatre just down from the Clock Tower – there's a beefburger place now isn't there? That was a Pathé film theatre. That was great. They had one at Victoria Station. I think it was for people waiting for trains. – **Geraldine Curran**

And then there was this place up in Kemptown called the Continentale and I went to Lourdes convent in Brighton and the nuns took us on the bus up to Paston Place where the Continentale was, to see *The Song of Bernadette*. We came in and the smell of humanity was awful and there were mice running around on the floor. It became very much an X cinema… it was a bit naughty. Nice girls didn't go to the Continentale. But there was another cinema, the Paris, which I went to with my sisters and the last film we saw was *Black Orpheus*. It was in Spanish I think. – **Geraldine Curran**

The Continentale ppened as the King's Cliff Cinema in 1920 in a converted Congregational church

There was a naughty cinema in Brighton we were told never to go to – I think it was called the Continentale – I was warned by my parents, don't you ever, ever go there! – **Rodney Patterson**.

ROBERT JEEVES

SUE CRAIG

FRANK FLOOD

ODEON
KEMP TOWN

(1934–1960)

LAST FILM SCREENED
Light up the Sky (1960) by Lewis Gilbert.

DID YOU KNOW?
During blackouts in WWII visitors to the cinema needed
to bring torches with them to see their way in.

SADLY, THE ODEON IN KEMPTOWN IS NOWADAYS more likely to be remembered for loss of life than for either the cinema itself or the films that played there. It was hit by one of a number of bombs dropped on the area by a lone German plane on the afternoon of 14 September 1940. Many among the audience were children as that morning's 'Mickey Mouse Club' screening had been carried over to the afternoon show, and the carnage was the worst seen in Brighton during the war. Published estimates of the death toll range from fourteen to fifty-five or more, with a larger number of injuries. Many Brightonians can still remember the event and its aftermath. The cinema was completely rebuilt and reopened just over three months later, in a remarkable display of wartime defiance.

The Odeon Kemp Town had first opened in February 1934 with a gala screening of Tom Walls' mildly amusing film of the Ben Travers farce: *A Cuckoo In The Nest*. Oscar Deutsch, founder of the Odeon chain, announced that the cinema would have a policy of showing only 'predominantly

In 1983 the cinema was renamed the City when it became a social centre run by the Bethany Fellowship

CHRIS HORLOCK

British' films, but this was quickly dropped in the face of commercial reality. It managed to survive the TV craze of the 1950s mainly because the Continentale, its only competitor on the Kemptown side of Brighton, had switched to showing largely European films, which would nowadays be termed 'art house'. In those days this was thought to be 'racy' programming, leaving the Odeon free to act as the third-run venue for the chain's mostly Hollywood fare. However, declining audiences saw it follow many of its rivals down the bingo route in November 1960. It closed as it had opened, with a mediocre British comedy *Light up the Sky!* starring Ian Carmichael and Tommy Steele.

The Saturday the Odeon got hit, my Mum was shopping in St James's Street. She left her shopping bag in the doorway of the Co-op and ran all the way to Whitehawk to see if we were safe. Later in the day, when the buses were running again, we took one to St James's Street and sure enough, her bag of shopping was still there! – **Eileen Alderson,** *Brighton Behind The Front***, 1990. QueenSpark Books.**

Originally the site of the Sassoon family's riding school, the Odeon cinema stood on the corner of St George's Road and Paston Place until January 1986, when the building was demolished to make way for Cavendish Court

SUE CRAIG

51

Top: Interior showing the damage sustained during the bomb attack of 14 September 1940
Bottom: The interior after post-bomb damage reconstruction, December 1940

"Sorry nurse, do you know where my daughter is?" Mum asked. "Her name is Michele, she was in the Odeon bombing and I would like to see her and if you can't find her then…" The injured had only just been brought in and not everyone had been identified. Michele wasn't on their list. We searched through the corridors until we heard her cheerful cry: "Mum, Marie!" – **story by Emily Atkinson-Dalton, age 11,** *Alt-History*, **2005. QueenSpark Books**

THE ROYAL PAVILION AND MUSEUMS, BRIGHTON & HOVE

ODEON
WEST STREET

(1937–1973)

FIRST FILM SCREENED

Either *Victoria the Great* starring Anna Neagle or *The Adventures of Tom Sawyer*. During the week's run of the latter there was a competition for a 'look-alike' of Tom Sawyer and the prize was a brand new bicycle.

DID YOU KNOW?

The Odeon West Street closed in 1973 and was demolished in 1990 along with the building next door, the ice rink SS Brighton, which had closed in October 1965.

'The Odeon in West Street opened in 1937. The Managers I remember were a Mr Self and then a Mr Sackier. Both appeared resplendent in 'black tie' in the evening from about six-thirty onwards greeting and talking to patrons. It was considered an honour if the Manager greeted you with a 'Good Evening'; they rarely spoke to members of the staff, instructions being passed on through the Chief of Staff, Mr Buttress, who came from the Palladium around the corner on the sea front. Mr. Buttress was a striking figure in his green uniform with tails. He was a strict disciplinarian, his word was law and woe betide the usherettes caught talking in whispers in the auditorium when a film was showing. He was, however, a very fair man and the sort of person to whom one could take one's problems. His son Leslie and a man named Bill Chard (who was a chain smoker of 'Churchman's Tenners'), together with two more doormen and two pageboys made up the front of house staff.

There were about twelve usherettes, the head usherette being my mother. A parade was held with all staff in the entrance foyer every day before the opening of the cinema and everyone was inspected for tidiness, make-up etc. No one giggled or spoke at these parades that were taken very seriously.

The Odeon, West Street in 1937

An interesting innovation during the war was the employment of a page girl, a very pretty blonde with blue eyes and very striking in her green uniform with a pillbox hat. Very much later she married Leslie Buttress. There were also the four Moore sisters: Rusty and Joan were usherettes, Vida was in the cash box, and the youngest, Pat, who later married an RAF pilot, was one of the ice cream sales girls who wandered around the auditorium during the shorts and second features, but *never* during the main feature. The Moore sisters used to live at the Railway Hotel just outside Brighton station.

There were many promotions for various films and the most striking that comes to mind was Cecil B De Mille's *North West Mounted Police* (1940) where all the usherettes were dressed up as Red Indian squaws complete with make-up, and the doormen were dressed up as Canadian Mounted Police officers. One should also remember that those days of the cinema were weekly events when patrons would dress up to 'go to the pictures' and there was a magic that does not exist today.

There was also a small tea lounge in the circle foyer where one could partake of a pot of tea, a toasted teacake, cakes etc. These could, if required, be taken to a person in the audience and there was always great amusement and a ripple of laughter when there was a crash as someone upset the tea tray.

The projection equipment was by British Thompson Houston, as was pretty standard in all Odeon cinemas. The Chief Projectionist was Mr. Chipperfield who came from the Regent and one of the junior projectionists, Luke Moneypenny, later went into management and finally ended up as the General Manager of the Odeon in Jersey, Channel Islands.

It is interesting to note that hard of hearing patrons were catered for, with several aisle seats in the rear stalls having plug points where a handset with a volume control could be plugged in. These were available free of charge at the cash desk. This is something that today's cinemas need and is one of the reasons I do not go to the cinema any more. The Odeon was built as a cinema and had no stage to speak of, but I do remember during a 'Wings for Victory' week a first rate show was put on, on the miniscule stage. One of the stars was Max Miller. – **John Wall**

I did go with my mother to see *Rock around the Clock* when I was ten and people were dancing in the aisles. There was a lot of vandalism, but it didn't happen when I was there, and there was an old lady who looked quite ancient but she suddenly got up in the aisles and started dancing as well. It was lovely, it was really a sort of atmosphere. This was in Brighton, I can't remember where, possibly the Odeon in West Street. I can't remember the exact cinema but I remember going with my mother to see it because she liked rock and roll. – **Geraldine Curran**

I went to see an Elvis Presley film. I think that was at the Odeon and I was too nervous to go on my own, so I asked

DUSASHENKA

The Odeon
shortly before its
demolition in 1990

my friend to come along. She loved Elvis Presley so every time something bad happened to Elvis, she was literally sobbing. I never liked Elvis films, the only decent one was *Jailhouse Rock* where he was a really good actor. I liked him when he was a real rock and roller, he was more exciting then. A bit like Cliff Richard; when they become decent and clean they are not so interesting! – **Geraldine Curran**

I remember we won a competition and we actually had a tour – we were taken round the back of the projection rooms at the Odeon, and we were told how, as they all smoked in the cinema, the screen had to be whitewashed every three months in order to keep the screen clear and get a good picture … Some of the cinemas were so bad they didn't do that, so you didn't have a very good quality picture – you'd get films on a brown screen. – **Bryan Moody**

AMY RILEY

REGENT
CINEMA

(1921–1974)

FIRST FILM SCREENED
Unknown, but most likely silent and in black and white
(the first partial talkie *The Jazz Singer* came out in 1927).

DID YOU KNOW?
Outside Boots on the Queens Road entrance
(near the Clock Tower) there is a small commemorative plaque
stating that this is the former location of the Regent cinema.

THE ROYAL PAVILION AND MUSEUMS, BRIGHTON & HOVE

T WAS THE EARLY 1920S AND ENGLAND WAS TRYING TO return to normal life; despite tough post-war economic times, there were plenty of advances in entertainment, with a boom in drinking, dancing, fashion – and the advent of luxury or 'super cinemas'.

The Regent cinema, unveiled on 27 July 1921, was situated on Queens Road and was one of the first that embraced new technology to develop a popular multifunction entertainment centre. Under the aegis of Provincial Cinematograph Theatres, work had begun on the site in 1920, destroying the medieval Unicorn Inn (built circa 1597) and creating a cinema that comfortably seated 2,024 at a cost of £400,000. Architect Robert Atkinson OBE adopted the art-deco style, which capitalised on cubic lines, geometric shapes and modern takes on ancient styles. Atkinson worked with a team of talented artists to complete the look: London artist Walter Bayes – who'd recently exhibited *The Underworld,* his wartime painting of East Londoners sheltering in a Tube station – on murals, Walpole Champneys on interiors, and Lawrence Preston on murals and the cinema's ornate proscenium (the decorated arch over the stage).

The main stage of the Regent cinema, Queens Road before the 1929 fire and featuring the elaborately painted proscenium arch

In keeping with its modern architecture, the cinema – which a few years later boasted a restaurant and orchestra, café and a sprung-floored dance hall (later a bingo hall) – kept ahead of the times by being the first Brighton cinema to install a sound system, as well as a Mighty Wurlitzer theatre organ, both in 1929.

The first film show in the new cinema – which opened on 27 July 1921 – is unknown, but it would have been silent and in black and white, as the first partial talkie *The Jazz Singer* came out in 1927. During its time the cinema screened its own local newsreel and may also have showed the one-minute government propaganda Topical Budget film, *Prince's 'Hustle' Visit to Brighton*

(1921), in which the Prince of Wales unveils an Indian troops' memorial. The Regent's last film was Liza Minnelli's *Cabaret* in 1973. The cinema closed its doors forever on 14 April 1973, and the building was demolished a year later.

The staff of the Regent Cinema, date unknown

'Ah, the Regent ballroom. What an experience for us Sunday evening dancing boys with the girls standing at the 'Cattle Market', waiting for a turn with whoever fancied it. The finest two bobs' worth in the town. (10 pence today!) ... Never again will a dance floor be so crowded with bodies against bodies, smooching to that favourite of the time, the Miller Medley. I met my wife-to-be out of the 'Cattle Market'. That would be 58 years ago. – **Ron Spicer**

I remember going to the Regent cinema as a boy in the mornings. We all belonged to the GB club (Gaumont British), and the club song went as follows:

We come along on Saturday morning, greeting everybody with a smile / We come along on Saturday morning, knowing that it's well worthwhile / We members of the GB club we all intend to be / Good citizens when we grow up, and champions of the free. / We come along on Saturday morning, greeting everybody with a smile, smile, smile / Greeting everybody with a smile. – **Henry (John) Stenhouse.**

On Wednesday afternoons, my father's half day, in the winter, we always went to the pictures. In the Regent they had budgerigars all along one side in a wire enclosure. We also had tea and toast on a tray, which must have been really dangerous as we had to pass the trays of tea along rows of people. – **Barbara Wykham.** *Back Street Brighton*, **1989 and 2007. QueenSpark Books**

At another cinema there was an event for me as a small boy which still seems remarkable. My mother and I were treated by my rich Aunt Olive to afternoon tea at the Regent complex (then near the corner of Queens Road and North Street). Tea was taken not in the restaurant on the floor below the ballroom, but whilst actually sitting in the stalls of the cinema watching a film. The shiny metal teapot and complements were on a huge shiny metal tray and we drank tea and ate toasted tea-cakes, surely to the annoyance of patrons around who were not having afternoon tea.

The 'pictures' were popular in those days, so popular that on a Saturday evening there would be a queue not only outside but another inside the Regent picture palace, patrons

The front of
the Regent cinema,
Queens Road, 1930

standing in a side gangway to watch the film whilst waiting for a seat. Film shows were not separate programmes, but continuous. So you would go in part way through the B-film and have to wait to see the beginning before you left. The programme would include a newsreel and sometimes a cartoon or a travelogue. Often popular tunes were played on a theatre organ which would have risen from the orchestra pit and glowed from within in pastel shades, whilst on the cinema screen a blob would hop from one word to the next in time with the music so the audience could sing along. My parents took me with them to the cinema every Saturday evening, except as a special treat when it was the Hippodrome variety theatre. – **John Knight,** *A Ha'p'orth of Sweets*. **1998. QueenSpark Books**

PETER BAILEY

The Regent,
summer 1952

I do remember, however, and quite clearly, the day she came home and announced joyfully that she had been offered a job at the soda fountain of the Regent Dance Hall, the ballroom attached to the Regent Cinema in West Street. A few years earlier the old Regent had been destroyed by fire, and by happy coincidence the new one was completed with the coming of the new 'Talking Pictures: All Talking – All Singing'. A new era in cinema history had begun. – **Sid Manville,** *Everything Seems Smaller*. **1989. QueenSpark Books**

Staff at the Regent, 1964

I had various jobs, mainly in cinemas: the Regent, the Palladium and the Curzon… I enjoyed the Regent; I was sales girl and usherette. You had to be smart as you had to go on parade every day before starting work. The manager would inspect us and tell us

HARRY ATKINS

where we were working for that day. We wore a very smart uniform: blue and white with silver buttons, also a forage cap with GB on the side: Gaumont British. It made you really feel important. – **Daphne Mitchell,** *Oh! What a Lovely Pier*. **1996. QueenSpark Books**

Jack and his friend persuaded us to go out to tea with them, then to the pictures. He said they couldn't dance in army boots. He didn't tell me it was because he couldn't dance, or that he didn't own a pair of shoes, but we agreed to go with them. We went for a meal in an ice cream parlour at the bottom of St James's Street, then on to the Regent cinema, after which we went to the station to see the boys on to their respective trains back to their bases. – **Olive Masterson,** *The Circle of Life*. **1986. QueenSpark Books**

The demolition of the Regent cinema, 1974

Again searching around
for work for short periods,
I found work that other
carpenters wouldn't take
on. After weeks had gone by
with no work I noticed a big
demolition job was going on
in North Street, Brighton,
also to shops in Queens
Road. After a few enquiries
I learned that a large cinema
was going to be built. As the
demolition came to an end

THE ROYAL PAVILION AND MUSEUMS, BRIGHTON & HOVE

and the rubble and rubbish was cleared away, the building
contractors moved in, plus tons and tons of steel girders,
stanchions and all the necessary tools and equipment. I kept
my eye on this job as the steel work was being erected and
eventually when I thought they must be ready to employ
carpenters I got an interview with the foreman who asked
me many questions.

The Regent cinema,
shortly before
demolition

When he was satisfied with my answers (of course these
foremen are experienced and they can tell by the way you
answer if you are a tradesman or not) he said I could start
the following Monday week. My first job was to make up four
carpenter's trestles (cutting stools). This was the test which
I have previously mentioned. I carried on working on this
site for many months, working in rough and wet conditions.
Eventually this site became the well-known Regent cinema in
Queens Road (the year being somewhere about 1921). Up till
about 1974 when it was demolished, the cinema and dance
hall continued to function and was very popular. – **Albert Paul,**
Hard Work and No Consideration. **1981. QueenSpark Books**

After a busy day one would go across to the Railway Bell
public house, by Brighton station, for a nice pint of beer,
cost four pence. On days off, three or four crewmen would
organise an outing. I used to go fishing with others in a boat
off Banjo Groyne, no engines then, we had to row out and
in. Sometimes we would go to dances and sometimes to
midnight films shown at the Regent cinema. – **Bert Hollick,**
Pullman Attendant. 1991. QueenSpark Books

When the Regent cinema opposite the Clock Tower opened, with its dance hall above, people came from all over the country, as it had the first sprung dance floor ever and was wonderful to dance on. – **Marjory Batchelor,** *A Life Behind Bars.* **1999. QueenSpark Books**

At the Regent we had about four or five projectionists – chief projectionist, second projectionist, third projectionist, fourth projectionist and rewind boy, we also had a lady projectionist, believe it or not … The Regent also had its ballroom on the top, and we used to go up there on a Saturday evening, into what was called the 'lime box' where all the lightings were, we used to help out by changing the colours. – **Peter Chitty**

When the Regent closed – the Regent was a really nice cinema – that was their roadshow theatre, so it ran all the 70mm big films – you could run a film for a year there on two shows a day – it was a beautiful building … I closed it, actually – the last night. I closed the gates on the old theatre and it never opened again – it was a bit run down, but it had

Site of the Regent, 1974

tremendous atmosphere – you don't get that in modern cinemas. – **John (former projectionist)**

We had a projectionist at the Regent come back one night; he'd obviously been to the pub during his break and he was slightly pie-eyed. He was in charge, and the idea was that you showed him you'd got the next part for the right film; so this chap brought out this film, he looked at it, laced it up on the projector – it was called *The Halls of Montezuma* (1950), a war film set in the Pacific – and we had a second feature, which was a film with Gene Tierney, a kind of psychological thriller. Anyway, time for changeover came – he changed over from the middle of a war film right into a black-and-white drama! – **Peter Chitty**

AMY RILEY

SAVOY
CINEMA

(1930–1999)

DID YOU KNOW?
The name of the Savoy cinema was changed to the ABC, the
Cannon, the Virgin and back to the ABC before closing in 1999.

Tourists heading down the narrow partly pedestrianised East Street, lured by the endless clothing and shoe shops, might not notice the two-story old-fashioned 1930s building at 75 East Street.

With the curved art-deco front and four doorways, the building's style might hint at its previous, more glamorous past, but it would probably take a local, who remembered going to the building during its heydays in the 1930s, 1940s and 1950s, to recall the popularity it held as a cinema, ballroom and restaurant.

The Savoy was a star herself and no stranger to reinvention, having boasted five name incarnations whilst a cinema, and a multitude of reconstructions; today, with the original building structure intact, it is home to Spearmint Rhino Rouge, a strip club, and Po Na Na, a nightclub.

The Savoy Cinema first opened its doors on 1 August 1930, exuding coolness and style with its 'off white' tiled exterior and Japanese interior. In 1930, Laurence Olivier, Buster

The Savoy, circa 1930

Crabbe (the actor who played Tarzan, Flash Gordon, and Buck Rogers), Rex Harrison, and Ethel Merman were unknowns. Betty Boop and Mickey Mouse were brand-spanking new. This stylish cinema, with its 2,300 seats, Westrex sound system, silk curtains, velvet-seated cinema, two restaurants, two cafés and a dance hall – and its own 300-car underground car park – was perfectly timed for the introduction of the talkies.

Over the course of the next sixty-nine years, this grand old dame played the glamorous hostess to the masses – with their innocent romances and illicit affairs, first kisses and first cigarettes – always offering the simple thrill of escaping from the world to sink into a film for a few hours.

The Savoy screened all the big hits of the time, such as *Wizard of Oz* and *Grease*, but it was in 1948 that the Savoy Cinema had her finest moment: *Brighton Rock*, the film based on Graham Greene's novel set in Brighton, had its world première in the cinema on 8 January at midnight.

Lady Luck smiled on the Savoy in the 1940s when the cinema was narrowly missed during a heavy bombing raid, which instead destroyed the Lyon and Hall music shop across the street. In May 1964, the cinema's windows were smashed by the Mods and the Rockers during the legendary Whitsuntide riots; the two-day fight was later immortalised in The Who's film *Quadrophenia* – with the cinema playing a cameo role.

Later decades saw attendances, and the cinema itself, decline; in 1999, the Savoy closed its doors to audiences forever.

'The site of the cinema has a history of leisure usage going back to the 1780s when it was Lamprell's Baths. In the 1820s Lamprell's nephew, Mr Brill took over the baths and they were rebuilt in 1869 to a design by Sir George Gilbert Scott. – **Editorial on www.mybrightonandhove.org.uk**

The Savoy in East Street was quite a posh place to go. Their staff were very smart and not all youngsters either. There was quite a few middle aged ladies doing usheretting. But they all had uniforms. Definitely. – **Diana Meeton**

WWII damage in Kings Road and the south end of East Street was severe. Most badly damaged was the Lyon and Hall music shop, which was located on the junction of Kings Road and East Street, opposite The Savoy cinema. This was Brighton's newest cinema at the time having opened 10 years earlier on the site of the old Brill's Baths. Many people will know it as the ABC, the acronym of its owners: Associated British Cinemas. – **Peter Groves**

The ABC, 1975

Youngsters come off the beach, change in the toilets, and you get puddles of water on your floor. They rinse their costumes under the tap and you get sand blocking the sinks. At the Colonnade, the Savoy – they used to come across the main road – you would go in and find pebbles everywhere.
– **Joan Parsons, *Jobs for Life*, 1995. Queen Spark Books**

I worked at the ABC as it was known then in the early 1990s. It was a lovely old building, it had gone to rot though, the main ballroom upstairs was still there, but the ceiling had partially collapsed and it was inhabited by pigeons. The huge number one screen had been closed for years, but the beautiful old silk curtains, enormous amounts of fabric, slightly tattered, were still hanging there. I remember thinking what a terrible waste it was. I also remember the characters who worked there. Mr Ruby was the manager, John the projectionist and especially a lady called Sylvia. She had worked there for donkey's years. When they were filming the riot scene in *Quadrophenia* in East Street, she panicked because she didn't realise it wasn't a real riot. – **ABC employee, contributor to www.mybrightonandhove.org.uk**

Left:
Brills Baths –
looking down
to Pool Valley, 1935.
Right: As the
ABC cinema, in
February 1967

THE ROYAL PAVILION AND MUSEUMS, BRIGHTON & HOVE

DUSASHENKA

25 BRIGHTON
MOVIES ON DVD

1 **BRIGHTON ROCK** (John Boulting 1948; available on Optimum DVD 2006). In which our razor-wielding anti-hero pursues Greeneian damnation through the mean streets of pre-war Brighton.

2 **THE ADVENTURES OF JANE** (Edward G. Whiting 1949; available on Odeon DVD 2008). In which our heroine loses some of her clothing while foiling a notorious gang of diamond smugglers.

3 **PENNY POINTS TO PARADISE** (Anthony Young 1951; available on BFI DVD 2009). In which our soon-to-be-Goons heroes are harassed by various comic attempts to steal their hard-earned pools winnings while on holiday.

4 **LADY GODIVA RIDES AGAIN** (Frank Launder 1951; available on Optimum DVD 2008). In which our heroine discovers that the glamour of beauty contests and filmmaking is not all it's cracked up to be.

5 **GENEVIEVE** (Henry Cornelius 1953; available on ITV DVD 2001). In which our heroes try to win a wager by racing from London to Brighton and back in somewhat elderly and unreliable vehicles.

6 **ONE GOOD TURN** (John Paddy Carstairs 1954; available on ITV DVD 2003). In which our hero attempts to save a children's home from closure and loses his trousers on a day at the seaside.

7 **THE BATTLE OF THE V-1** (Vernon Sewell 1958; available on Simply Media DVD 2006). In which our heroes battle doodlebugs while parts of Portslade and Shoreham stand in for Nazi-occupied Europe during WWII.

8 **BE MY GUEST** (Lance Comfort 1965; available on Simply Media DVD 2008). In which our hero and his parents move from London to take over a Brighton boarding house, and he then attempts to become a teen pop sensation.

9 **OH! WHAT A LOVELY WAR** (Richard Attenborough 1969; available on Paramount DVD 2006). In which our WWI heroes embark from the piers only to discover that a sing-song is scant compensation for being Lions Led By Donkeys.

10 **LOOT** (Silvio Narizzano 1971; available on Cinema Club DVD 2005). In which our larcenous anti-heroes hide their ill-gotten gains in a coffin and Woodvale Cemetery proves to be an ideal Ortonesque location.

11 **DIE SCREAMING, MARIANNE** (Pete Walker 1971; available on Odeon DVD 2009). In which our heroine goes on the run to Brighton before deciding that being a nightclub 'hostess' is a bad idea.

12 **CARRY ON AT YOUR CONVENIENCE** (Gerald Thomas 1971; available on ITV DVD 2003). In which the entire staff of WC Boggs & Son (you get the general idea) go to Brighton for the annual works' outing.

13 **CARRY ON GIRLS** (Gerald Thomas 1973; available on ITV DVD 2003). In which the sleepy seaside town of Fircombe hosts a titanic clash between the forces of beauty pagentry and militant feminism.

14 **QUADROPHENIA** (Franc Roddam 1979; available on Universal DVD 2006). In which our hero discovers Mod, leaves home, pops pills, fights, loves, loses, sleeps on the beach and goes over the edge.

15 **MONA LISA** (Neil Jordan 1986; available on Starz DVD 2006). In which our hero goes on the run, has a memorable ruckus on the pier and learns some sobering facts about What Women Want.

16 **THE FRUIT MACHINE** (Philip Saville 1988; available on Network DVD 2007). In which our heroes decamp from Liverpool to Brighton in order to escape a crime scene and discover their sexual identities.

17 **DIRTY WEEKEND** (Michael Winner 1993; available on Universal DVD 2006). In which Michael Winner (of sexist vigilante movie fame) becomes a self-declared 'feminist' by making a sexist movie about a female vigilante.

18 **THE END OF THE AFFAIR** (Neil Jordan 1999; available on UCA DVD 2004). In which our hero pursues a Greeneian 'dirty weekend' of the soul in an allegedly wartime Brighton.

19 **CIRCUS** (Rob Walker 2000; available on UCA DVD 2004). In which our hero discovers that tangling with Britflick gangsters is a bad idea – and that the Brighton naturist beach is apparently beside the West Pier.

20 **ME WITHOUT YOU** (Sandra Goldbacher 2001; available on Momentum DVD 2002). In which our heroines discover themselves via university, sex, drugs and breakdown before ending up older, wiser and (evidently) wealthier.

21 **SUMMER RAIN** (Jonathan Glendening 2002; available on Eureka DVD 2006). In which our heroines discover themselves via sex, drugs and rock 'n' roll (but not university) over the course of a Long Hot Summer.

22 **WIMBLEDON** (Richard Loncraine 2004; available on Universal DVD 2006). In which our hero is a tennis player from Brighton having predictably less success than the rising US star he gets involved with.

23 **MIRRORMASK** (Dave McKean 2005; available on Sony DVD 2006). In which our teenage heroine discovers that Embassy Court at its most down-at-heel is actually the gateway to another world entirely.

24 **LONDON TO BRIGHTON** (Paul Andrew Williams 2006; available on Momentum DVD 2007). In which our heroine attempts to escape from prostitution and violence in London with a young runaway girl in tow.

25 **ANGUS, THONGS AND PERFECT SNOGGING** (Gurinder Chadha 2008; available on Paramount DVD 2008). In which our heroine gets to grips with love, pain and unsuitable underwear against a backdrop which proves that Brighton is trendier than Eastbourne.